Home Inc.
Publishing

First Printing - 1990
Second Printing - 1994

Roxie Cawood Gibson

Printed in the U.S.A.

ISBN   0-9640392-4-9

INTRODUCTION

As an individual and family therapist the subject of death frequently surfaces as a fear and mystery within the hearts and minds of my patients. At last I have an exciting readable and illustrated resource by two of my special friends to share with others. **Hey God! What Is Death?**, bridges the gap between fear and uncertainty and explains so clearly the hope and joy which lies before us as we look to joining the presence of God and our loved ones.

Death does **not** have to be a fear nor that great of a mystery! Our faith is designed to give us hope and peace. But not until someone can wrestle with the issues as Roxie has these past three years, and comes to a clear expression of the meaning of that hope and joy, do we really personalize the gift of life eternal which God has promised for us.

Written on Christmas day, 1989, Roxie has given us a gift which will last a life time and for hereafter!

As a student of psychology and theology, I have read numerous books on this subject. But until now, we have not had such a powerful and meaningful tool that is both simple and profound.

This volume leaves us speechless and at the same time enables us to understand and express our feelings of comfort in knowing and understanding what death really is through faith in our Lord Jesus Christ.

As Paul Harvey would say . . . now we truly know the rest of the story. Death is not the end. Death is moving to a new and wonderful beginning.

DON H. HIGHLANDER, JR., PH.D.

This book is
dedicated
with utmost love to our
Lord and Saviour,
Jesus Christ

and

with special love for

my sweet Mama,

Leesha,

Chris,

Papa Cooper,

and Dan.

Hey, God!
It's really neat
to know You're
always there
to listen to
me and to
know that

-1-

You love me
just

like
I

am!

-z-

I'm so glad
you're my
friend and
I can talk
to you
anytime!

I tell my friends
about you, God.
I tell them
you're the
oldest and
best friend
I have.

I tell them about
Psalm 139, where it
says that you knew
me even before my
Mom and Dad
did. Some of them
don't believe this,
God, but they
will after they
get to know
you better.

You know, God,
when I grow
up, I want
to spend my
whole life
telling other
people about
You!

They get excited
about Batman
and that stuff,
but just wait
'til I tell them
about all the
things YOU
can do!

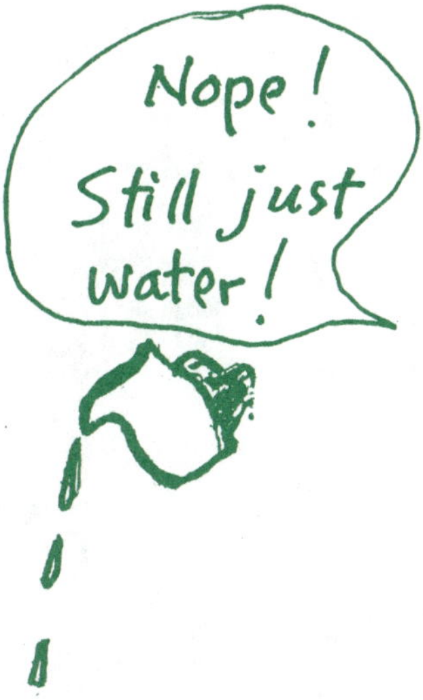

I'll bet Batman couldn't turn water into wine, could he, God?

anyway, God, if
I'm going to tell
other people about
You, You're
going to have
to help me a
whole lot with
things <u>I</u> don't
understand...

- 14 -

right now I'm
having trouble
understanding
about death.
You see, God, someone
I love very much
died, and I
really do miss
her.

When I ask big
people about death,
they give me
answers I don't
understand, and
tell me we'll talk
about it later.
Well, I know
what _later_ means.--

it's the same
as never!

So I went to
Mr. Webster again
thinking he
Could help me,
and you know
what, God?
He knows even
less than I
do!

- 20 -

He said death
means extinction
of life, decease,
cause of decease,
demise - - -
now who could
understand
all that?

-23-

Then I looked up
all the other words
people use in talking
about death ...
casket, coffin,
funeral, embalm,
bury ... those words
are so scary and
sad, it's no wonder
nobody wants
to talk about it!

Well, then I looked in the Bible and read that if Adam and Eve hadn't disobeyed you, we wouldn't have to know about death.

Now that made
me mad , because
it really would be
neat to stay here
on earth forever
and not have my

family or friends

die.

You see, God, I
really like things
the way they are
now. I love your
mountains, streams,
twinkling stars,

and having
Mr. Moon come
up at night and
follow me everywhere
I go.

-30-

You know, God,
your earth
is a
very special
place!

Well, I didn't
stay mad at
Adam and Eve
long, God, 'cause
I remembered how
bad we all are
(forgive me, God,
for the bad things
I do).

Then I read in
the Bible about the
beautiful place
You have prepared
for us to go when
we die (Mr. Webster
said that "prepared"
means "made ready"
--- he did a little
better this time).

(On this page, draw
what <u>you</u> think Heaven
will be like)

Does this mean
that dying means
moving? Gee, how
easy that is to
understand.
I don't need any
help with the word
" move ". Everyone
knows that means
to change houses.

-38-

So "dying" is really just moving from our house here to your house in Heaven. Well, I like that word "moving" better! Thanks for helping me with this, God.

You know, God,
the bad part
about moving
is that when
someone you love
moves, you are
sad because
you miss them.

But it helps to
remember that
someday we will
all move, and then
we can stay with
each other and
with you forever...
and forever is
a l-o-n-g time!

Well anyway, God,
when we move in
with you, we
won't have to
pack anything
because we've
already sent
the things
we need.

- 45 -

Now I know what
you meant when
you said, "Store up
for yourself treasures
in Heaven". I'm
going to start
working on that, God.
I'll help feed the
hungry and go
visit people who
are sick or
lonely.

—46—

But most of all, God,
I'll tell others about
You and how much
You love them.
I'll tell them
how you sent
your only Son,
Jesus, to earth
to die for us.

- 48 -

If they will
just believe in
Jesus, they won't
have to die ---

they'll just
move to Heaven
with you!

- 49 -